Devon Smugglers

The truth behind the fiction

Robert Hesketh

Bossiney Books · Launceston

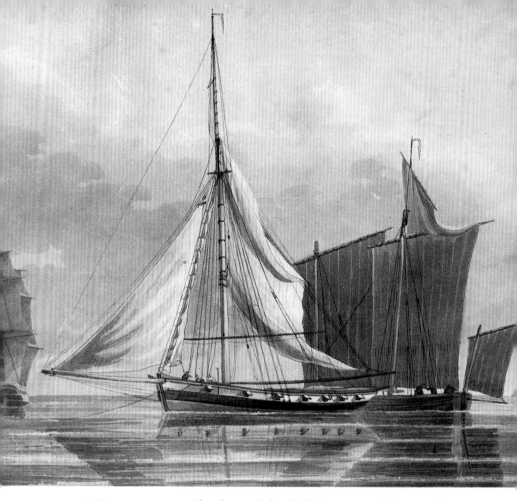

A Revenue cutter with a lugger behind. This was a typical smuggling vessel which could well have been taken as a prize

This reprint 2010

First published 2007 by Bossiney Books Ltd
Langore, Launceston, Cornwall PL15 8LD
www.bossineybooks.com

ISBN 978-1-899383-93-1

Acknowledgements

The historic prints on the following pages were supplied by Mssrs John Maggs of Falmouth: 1, 7, 11, 15, 22, 27, 29 and 32. All photographs are by the author except that on page 31. Other illustrations are from the publishers' own collection.

Printed in Great Britain by R Booth Ltd, Penryn, Cornwall

Introduction

From 1700 to 1850 smuggling constituted one of Devon's chief sources of wealth. Indeed, smuggling – or 'free trade' as its practitioners preferred to call it – was at that time a major industry throughout Britain, involving a network of shippers, financiers and distributors, reaching from the humblest strata of society to the highest. Perhaps a quarter of Britain's import/export trade was illegal. For some commodities, tea in particular, the figure may have been as high as two thirds.

Geography fostered Devon's seafaring traditions, its host of sailors, boat builders and fishermen, who provided the skilled men and vessels for smuggling. Devon's long, indented coastlines, north and south, are well suited for landing illicit cargoes unobserved. Moreover, the county's westerly position made it remote from central government control, especially before turnpike roads and railways arrived. The sea gave Devon good communications with its main suppliers of contraband – the Channel Islands and Brittany.

Poverty and a thirst for adventure meant there were plenty of men willing to flout Customs and Excise duties widely regarded as unjust and unwarranted. Few Devonians regarded smuggling as a crime; many benefited from it and thus supported it, which greatly reduced the risk of capture for smugglers. In places such as Beer, Sidmouth and Kingsand many people were actively involved in smuggling and few would dare betray a smuggler for fear of ostracism and reprisal.

Support for smuggling extended to the county establishment of clergy, justices and even the aristocracy. These pillars of society frequently connived in buying contraband, financing smuggling operations and protecting smugglers from the law.

It is hardly surprising smuggling was popular. To some it brought considerable wealth. For many more, it raised their incomes above subsistence level. It also brought luxuries such as brandy, snuff and tobacco within the reach of almost everyone.

Rudyard Kipling, with his keen instinct for popular history and sentiment, summarised the situation well in 'Smuggler's Song':

> Them that asks no questions isn't told a lie,
> Watch the wall my darling, while the Gentlemen go by!
> Five and twenty ponies
> Trotting through the dark –
> Brandy for the Parson,
> 'Baccy for the Clerk...

His Majesty's Government sought to finance a long series of wars – principally with the smugglers' main business partners, the French – through punitive taxes on luxury goods, whilst the smugglers strove to supply those goods cheaply and illegally through 'free trade'. In the protracted struggle between smugglers and the Law, the smugglers generally had the best of things, especially in the early stages of the conflict, when contraband was often landed with impunity on open beaches such as Sidmouth, Exmouth and Torquay, or even surreptitiously offloaded at ports under the very noses of Customs officers.

More often than not, the smugglers outwitted or outmanoeuvred their opponents. The picture of the clever underdog fooling the dull-witted authorities is part of the enduring appeal of smuggling. It is not the whole truth, as smugglers also resorted to violence and intimidation – though this was less the case in the West Country than in Kent and Sussex, where large criminal gangs controlled much of the activity.

Certainly, the preventive services, including the crews of Revenue cutters and the Royal Navy, made life increasingly difficult for smugglers, especially after the formation of the Coastguard in 1822. However, vast quantities of smuggled goods continued to pour into England until the mid 19th century, when the government itself adopted 'free trade' as an article of economic faith.

'Free trade', the very cause smugglers claimed to espouse (or the excuse they made for their crimes), ended the classic era of smuggling. Profits evaporated when taxes on spirits, tea and tobacco were slashed.

How smuggling grew and prospered

Along the English coast, smuggling began in medieval times with the illegal export of the nation's main source of wealth, wool, which carried a heavy duty. 'Owling' (wool smuggling) opened England's textile industry to keen foreign competition and was severely punished. Owlers risked having their left hands cut off by a law of 1566. This was reduced to transportation in the early 18th century.

Illegal export of tin from the county's mines was a larger feature of smuggling in Devon. Until 1838, the law required all tin to be sold through Devon's Stannary towns – Chagford, Ashburton, Tavistock and Plympton. As Devon's tin production declined during the 17th and 18th centuries, other opportunities were found by smugglers to export manufactures, such as woollen cloth and needles. These fetched good prices in France.

When a shortage of gold struck France in 1784, obliging English smugglers took boatloads of gold across the Channel, despite the fact that the two nations were at war. Later, Bonaparte relied heavily on smuggled English gold to pay his troops.

Illegally importing goods became the mainstay of 'free trade' after 1700 and grew through the 18th century, despite increasingly severe penalties. From 1718, the Hovering Acts were aimed at vessels loitering along the coast with intent to offload smuggled goods. Boats carrying more than four oars and suspect cargoes could be seized and sawn into three pieces.

The 1736 and 1746 Smuggling Acts escalated penalties. The names of known smugglers were published in the *London Gazette* in 1746. Any gazetted smuggler who did not surrender within forty days was automatically subject to the death penalty. This action broke the violent Groombridge and Hawkhurst smuggling gangs in the south-east of England. Their leaders were hung in chains.

However, these drastic Acts had little impact in Devon. The authorities had great difficulty in securing any convictions against smugglers, who usually enjoyed the backing of local juries. Few smugglers suffered the death penalty. Where they did, it was usually for murder rather than smuggling, as in the case of the *Lottery* (page 16). Fines, imprisonment or forced service in the Navy were the main risks run by smugglers – though shipwreck was a greater danger still.

War and smuggling went hand in hand, for the government's main sources of revenue to wage war were Customs and Excise duties. Indeed, the classic smuggling period began in the late 17th century with William III's wars against Louis XIV's France.

Smuggling thrived as duties were repeatedly raised through the 18th century's many imperial wars and reached its zenith during the protracted Revolutionary and Napoleonic Wars.

When at war, the Royal Navy had more vital concerns than seizing contraband. War also weakened the preventive services as sailors were recruited from the Revenue cutters for naval service. Equally, the Army was obliged to send men abroad to fight rather than keep them at home on such duties as coast watching. These wartime necessities were no doubt welcomed by smugglers who (when not forced to serve in His Majesty's ships as an alternative punishment to prison) enjoyed much more freedom from detection when Britain was at war.

Largely because it insisted on imposing duties on goods sold to the American colonies, whilst refusing them full political rights, the government was confronted with the American War of Independence. Desperately short of fighting men, it offered a deal to smugglers under the 1782 Act of Oblivion. A convicted smuggler who could find one landsman and one seaman for His Majesty's armed forces would escape a penalty up to a £500 fine. In exchange for two of each, he could avoid any legal punishment, however great.

During war and peace, smuggling amounted to a large industry, though many of the operators (especially in the West Country) were small fry. In 1783, amidst the wars with France, George Bishop estimated that 60,000 of England's youngest and ablest men were involved in smuggling, along with 100,000 women and children who distributed contraband:

> There are many thousands of sailors employed in this illicit
> traffick, many of whom are victualled and cloathed, and
> their vessels repaired in foreign countries, who would
> otherwise become fishermen, and other useful members of
> the community, thereby greatly enriching the sea coasts...
> The smuggling-cutters are not only large, full of men and
> well armed, but so well constructed for sailing that
> seldom one of them is captured... whilst great numbers
> are employed in removing smuggled goods from one part
> of the country to another... Smuggling is arrived to a
> height unprecedented in this or (perhaps) any other nation
> in Europe.

Bishop was not alone in his estimate of the prevalence of smuggling. That same year (1783), a parliamentary committee reported 300 English vessels continuously involved in smuggling – in effect, a second merchant navy. This did not include foreign smacks, post office vessels, East Indiamen, fishing boats and even vessels of His Majesty's Navy – all of which were known to take a hand in illicit trading.

The government had created the conditions for smuggling. By 1815 – the year of Waterloo – an incredible 1425 items were subject to duty, including such unlikely commodities as Leghorn hats and playing cards (both of which were recovered in Revenue hauls), as well as the better known spirits, lace, silk, snuff and tobacco. Among the smugglers of Kent, Sussex and Hampshire – who were both more numerous and more inclined to violence than the men of Devon and Cornwall – Dutch geneva, otherwise known as gin or Hollands, was a major smuggled commodity.

A view across Torbay, with Brixham in the foreground

In Devon, French brandy was the market leader in what was quite possibly the county's most profitable industry. In 1783 excisemen estimated that half the smuggled brandy in England came via Devon and Cornwall. That estimate was a startling four million gallons (eighteen million litres) annually, or six bottles for every adult in the country. Like gin, brandy could yield a profit of 400-500%, amply justifying the risks involved in a smuggling run. Profits on tobacco, which was often hidden in bales of cloth, sewn into clothing or boots (hence 'bootlegging') or disguised as rope, sometimes reached 1000% during the Napoleonic Wars.

The government had the essential remedy in its own hands – to cut duty radically. However, because of the exigencies of war, this was only done intermittently and piecemeal. When Pitt halved the duty on wine, smuggling was undermined. Similarly, when he cut duty on tea from 125% to a mere 12^1/2%, tea smuggling was all but eliminated at a stroke. But with income tax politically unacceptable to the ruling classes (who would have paid most of it) taxes on goods in general rose higher and higher and smuggling became well established. It was an industry with recognisable family firms such as the Carters in West Cornwall and the Rattenburys and Mutters in East Devon.

Smuggling, as a modern businessman would readily appreciate, involved team work. There were four branches to the trade, each essential to the smuggling operation. The venturers put up the money to finance the business. The crews of smuggling vessels as well as local traders and farmers often bought small shares in a smuggling run but the main shareholders or venturers were naturally men of substance. They particularly preferred to stay in the background, especially if they were magistrates or clergymen such as the Reverends Stapleton and Mundy, smuggling vicars of East Budleigh.

Next, there was the captain and crew. Their vessel might be a fishing boat, a fast rowing boat known in Devon and Cornwall as a gig, a regular trading vessel or a purpose built lugger. Their skill and daring was widely admired, as this extract from Edward Pelham Brenton's *The Naval History of Great Britain* (1823) shows:

> These are men as remarkable for their skill in seamanship as for their audacity in the hour of danger, they are beyond competition our best pilots and fore and aft sailors…they are hardy, sober and faithful to each other, beyond the generality of seamen; and where a shipwreck occurs, have been known to perform deeds not exceeded in any country in the world.

Not surprisingly, the Royal Navy was eager to take convicted smugglers like Jack Rattenbury of Beer on board – though Jack and his friends were usually less than willing to serve. Among the many amusing – and often embroidered – accounts in Rattenbury's *Memoirs of a Smuggler* (1837) are his escapes from the Navy and others who would have forced him back into the Service. Another use that both the French and English authorities found for smugglers was as spies, their illegal trade being good cover for intelligence gathering. Immunity from prosecution was probably part of the deal.

Rattenbury also mentions the third part of the smuggling team, the merchants who supplied the contraband. These gentlemen were well established on the Channel Islands, which Jack often visited. Although some Devon smugglers bought brandy direct from Nantes on the Atlantic coast of France, the ideally placed Channel Islands, free of Customs by an ancient charter, were the usual source of supply in the early days of Devon smuggling.

The bi-lingual Channel Islands merchants cultivated their French contacts and built great storehouses for contraband, as well as utilising caves. Naturally, they deeply resented attempts in 1717, 1720 and

1722 to establish a Custom House on the Islands similar to the Custom Houses in Exeter and Dartmouth. In 1767 an Act of Parliament restricted the Channel Islands trade and a Custom House was finally established on Guernsey. Knowing well how profitable smuggling was to his nation's economy and how it undermined the finances of his English rival, the French king promptly made Roscoff a free port.

Conveniently situated on the Breton coast opposite Plymouth, Roscoff grew apace and offered large warehouses. The English and especially the western Cornish, who found Breton easy to learn because it was so like their own language, were soon established as traders and residents. A well-known sight was Harry Carter of the notorious West Country smuggling family and a staunch Methodist, holding open air services on Roscoff Quay. John Wesley would not have been amused. Somewhat unusually for an authority figure of his day, Wesley not only condemned the slave trade (in which Britain led the world) but smuggling too, as his *Word to a Smuggler* (1767) and repeated exhortations to his flocks make clear.

Despite the new Custom House, the Channel Islands smuggling trade recovered and continued to thrive down to 1808, when the Islands were brought into line with mainland Customs and Excise. Devon smugglers largely switched to merchants in Roscoff, Morlaix and St Malo, despite the Royal Navy's campaign to blockade French ports.

The fourth element in the smuggling team was the landing and distribution squad on shore. Rattenbury glided over this essential element in the business, because his son was still an active smuggler when he wrote his *Memoirs*.

Landing the contraband undetected was the first task. Ensuring that 'the coast was clear' – a smuggling term now in general usage – was thus a key part of the shore team's job. It is well described in *Beer in Smuggling Times* by Arthur J Chapple, whose family has lived in Rattenbury's home village for generations. With the whole community watching the watchers – the Riding Officers on shore and the Revenue cutters at sea – intelligence gathering was made much easier and more efficient.

A skipper running contraband would certainly not want to be intercepted and have his vessel 'rummaged'. Signalling that the coast was clear or not, for instance by smoke, fire or lights, was effective as long as visibility was fair. Such signalling was punishable as a crime, so less obvious methods were devised. One was a spout lantern, which cast a narrow beam out to the smugglers at sea, but was invisible from the land. Another was to hang a red garment on a suitably placed washing line, or to have a man wearing a coloured coat ride his horse along the cliff path.

If the coast was clear, the landing party met the smuggling vessel at a pre-arranged rendezvous, often a secluded cove such as Brandy Cove between Shaldon and Maidencombe. A moonless winter's night was ideal for concealment. Though such conditions made landing more difficult and dangerous, they also discouraged the Revenue cutters from leaving port.

The landing party usually consisted of local labourers who knew the area intimately and would be well paid for a night's work. Their task was to unload the vessel as quickly and quietly as possible and take away or hide the incriminating evidence.

At the more inaccessible coves, men had to haul the contraband up steep cliffs. A farm gate attached by ropes to a winch was used for this purpose at Salcombe Regis – until the ropes snapped and a smuggler fell to his death.

An alternative from some beaches was to carry the goods up narrow cliff paths, as described in J Meade Faulkner's Dorset smuggling novel, *Moonfleet* (1898). Brandy was often borne in two or four gallon casks called ankers, slung fore and aft over a man's shoulders with rope – customarily provided by the thoughtful merchants, who also supplied other smuggling equipment. At the cliff top, a team of sure-footed donkeys or ponies would be waiting. However, at some landing places such as Torre Abbey Sands (Torquay was then just a small fishing community) the animals could take the loads directly from the beach.

With their hooves muffled, the pack animals processed silently through the night to deliver their goods to customers or hiding places, ranging from hollow trees to church towers, farmers' barns, hidden wall cavities in inns, quarries, caves and specially constructed pits.

Of course, the revenue men might suspect that donkeys or ponies were being used to move smuggled goods, but it was hard to prove a case against men who ostensibly made their livelihoods as seaweed gatherers or carters. Jack Rattenbury found an excellent colleague in turf cutter Abraham Mutter, who had his own horse and cart and a list of legitimate customers. Mutter later recruited his brother and son for the smuggling business. The family – reputedly the last to make a living from smuggling in the old era – is remembered in Mutter's Moor

A schooner with a smack in the foreground, both of them typical coastal trading vessels of the early nineteenth century

in Otterton parish and Mutter's Wood in Yarcombe parish.

Landing and hiding places can often be located and visited today and are described later in this book. Sceptics will dismiss rumours that many of these places, such as Bovey House near Beer, are haunted. However, such invented or embroidered stories did much to deter prying eyes in a more credulous age.

Another deterrent was the batman. Like the American TV hero, batmen commonly wore black cloaks and even masks on occasion, but their task was to protect smugglers with their swingle bats and other weaponry, including firearms in some cases.

Sometimes, the coast was not clear and a landing had to be postponed or cancelled. This left the problem of what to do with the contraband. A solution increasingly used, especially when the preventive services became more vigilant and efficient after the Napoleonic Wars, was to 'sow the crop'.

This meant tying barrels containing spirits and sometimes other contraband to lengths of rope, weighting them and sinking them at sea. The buoyancy of the spirits made the barrels float above the sea bed. They could be recovered with care using grappling hooks or even specially trained dogs.

Crab and lobster fishing, which involves hauling up wicker pots marked by cork floats, provided the ideal disguise for 'working the crop'. This was the smugglers' term for recovering the barrels, which could be hidden under a legitimate catch of fish. Although the brandy barrels were tarred to prevent contamination of their contents with salt water, it was best to recover them within a few days for they inevitably leaked in time and the spoilt spirit had to be sold cheaply as 'stinkibus'. Another danger was that the barrels might work loose in a storm and be lost.

Smugglers developed other methods of bringing their cargoes home safely. One was to hide contraband under false decks and bulkheads, or in specially constructed water tanks with false sides. A hollow mast also provided extra storage space, whilst various disguises were used for carrying goods undetected. One was to weave tobacco into ship's rope. Kingsand women carried bladders filled with brandy under their skirts – but the *mores* of the time inhibited a full body search!

Struggle with the preventive services

We have seen that Devon's smugglers enjoyed several advantages in their struggle with the preventive services. In the first place, there were many more smugglers than preventive men. In the early and mid 18th century in particular, the smugglers often appeared better organised, carrying on their trade with impunity. For instance, in December 1760, 25 men from Beer, mounted on horses, took a train of 30 pack animals loaded with contraband tea into Exeter. They rode unmolested through the city and continued on their way. Six years later, 40 smugglers and their pack train drove off a force of Customs men, led by William Hunt. Hunt suffered a dislocated shoulder in the encounter.

Smugglers enjoyed strong support in the local community, often including the rich and powerful such as Lord Rolle, who eventually became Rattenbury's patron and gave him a pension. Another gentleman smuggler was Sir William Courtenay of Powderham, who perjured himself in 1833 and was sentenced to transportation. It is significant he committed this offence whilst defending naval colleagues on smuggling charges.

Devon was a smuggling county. Convicting a Devonian on smuggling charges within the county was hard. There was a better chance of gaining a conviction if the accused was tried in London, where the jury did not know him. The Dartmouth Revenue Collector wrote to London:

> We think it almost impossible to convict by a Devonshire
> Jury who are composed of smugglers and the greatest part
> of them are either smugglers or always ready to assist them.

Among the smugglers were many skilled sailors. Like Jack Rattenbury, they were generally bred to the sea from an early age and knew their craft and the local waters better than anyone. Further proof of their skill comes from Rattenbury's *Memoirs*. Seeing a troopship in danger he boarded her and – acting as pilot – brought her to safety. Awarding Rattenbury twenty guineas, the Captain advised him to have a handbill printed (Jack was illiterate), describing his brave exploit. The handbill so impressed Lord Rolle that he several times acted as Rattenbury's protector.

Often outmatched in seamanship, the Revenue had some advantage in its beautifully crafted cutters (see page 2). Built for speed and not comfort, these vessels carried a huge spread of sail, aided by an extra long bowsprit. To maintain this advantage, the length of bowsprits was limited by law on all other vessels; for the same reason the number of oars a gig could legally carry was limited. Smugglers consequently designed their cutters with more sail aloft.

Eventually, the Revenue cutter service mustered over 50 vessels of nearly 200 tons each. Commanded by Lieutenants of the Royal Navy, the total force was some 1300 men. It was a tough job, which often included a night guard duty in an open rowing boat.

In 1784, there were six Revenue cutters based in Cornwall and four in Devon. This was not a large number to patrol such a long coastline – and all the Devon cutters were stationed on the south coast. They were the *Ranger*, based at Plymouth with a crew of 21; *Wasp*, also stationed at Plymouth with 20 on board; plus *Alarm* at Exeter with 21 men and *Spider* at Dartmouth with a crew of 28.

The main compensation for the hardships and dangers of joining a Revenue cutter, or any other part of the preventive service, was prize money from captured contraband. 'Rewards for seizures' as it was also called were often on a lavish scale. Sums of £1000 distributed between the officers and men at a coastguard station after a successful haul were by no means unusual.

For some, the opportunities to smuggle under the cloak of the law were too much to resist. In 1825, the entire crew of the Revenue cutter *Rose* was dismissed for smuggling tobacco and in 1832 the crew of the cutter *Nimble* was dismissed for smuggling spirits at Exmouth, where they had been stationed many years.

The problem of corruption among the law enforcers was much more extensive than these cases suggest and it extended to the judiciary. As long ago as 1675, Joseph Trevers wrote:

> It is well-known that smugglers…have oft times great interest with the magistrates; and being purse proud do not value what they spend to ingratiate themselves with persons of authority to [discredit] all such as discover their fraudulent dealings, or else by bribes to stop their mouths. The smugglers are not only acquainted with some lawyers and clerks, but they make good interest with the under-sheriffs in the counties where they drive their trade… some of them will take part with the offenders, instead of executing the law against them.

In 1743, the zealous Collector Warren Lisle, whose sloop *Cholmondeley* was based at Exeter, claimed over-optimistically that Revenue vessels were 'able to attack the smugglers in every little creek along the coast of Devenshire (sic) and Cornwall.' A sadder and a wiser man by 1782, he reported to the Prime Minister that the four Revenue cutters operating between St Alban's Head in Dorset and Berry Head near Brixham '…agree with the smugglers and content themselves with a small part from the smuggler, suffer the greater part to be run on shore.' This suggests that bribery – which was widespread at all levels of society in the 18th century – was another successful tactic for the smugglers, who could afford to lose a proportion of their cargoes, given their high profit margins.

Even when the Revenue apparently triumphed, one is sometimes left wondering about their integrity. In 1819 the Revenue cutter *Sprightly* chased a French row galley (a Gallic version of a gig) for four hours. The smugglers threw 200 kegs of brandy overboard, a ploy which, as well as lightening the vessel and making it faster, often diverted the Revenue men completely from the chase. However, despite all their efforts, on this occasion the smugglers were forced ashore at Exmouth and six of them were captured. Sixty-eight abandoned brandy kegs were recovered and sent to the Custom House at Topsham. What happened to the rest is not explained.

A fishing smack by day, a smuggler the next dark night

Intimidation was another tactic employed by smugglers. In 1732 the Plymouth Tide Surveyor who supervised the Landguard was murdered 'about the running of brandy'. Two men were hung in chains at Crabtree on the Laira estuary for the crime. Occasional murder continued. In 1787, two excisemen were murdered at Roncombe Gate south of Honiton (near Farway on what is now the B3174). A free pardon and a £200 reward were offered to anyone supplying information leading to the killers' conviction.

High cliffs seem to have been a particular hazard for Customs men. In 1775 Henry Mugford, the Waiter and Searcher at Brixham 'fell over a cliff' and was drowned. Ten years later, Richard Cullin met his death under similar circumstances. In Branscombe churchyard between Beer and Sidmouth is the following epitaph:

> Here lieth the Body of Mr John Hurley, Custom House Officer of this Parish. As He was endeavoring to extinguish some Fire made between Beer and Seaton as a Signal to a Smuggling Boat then off at Sea He fell by some means or other from the Top of the Cliff to the Bottom by which He was unfortunately Killed. This unhappy Accident happened

15

the 5th day of August in the Year of our Lord 1755. *Aetatis suae* 45. He was an active and Diligent Officer and very inoffensive in his life and Conversation.

Sometimes, it was not the case of a lone officer mysteriously falling over a cliff, but an armed confrontation between smugglers and preventive men. The smugglers were well prepared for trouble. In the 1780s, three heavily armed smuggling vessels were known to make regular trips between Guernsey and South Devon.

Ranger was a lugger of over 200 tons and carried 22 guns and a crew of 100. She was built at Cawsand, the notorious smuggling village on the Cornish border, which, with Kingsand in Devon dominated the lucrative smuggling trade in Plymouth Sound. Somewhat smaller was the *Dogger Bank*, whilst the smallest, *Swift*, was nonetheless formidable with 16 guns and a crew of 50.

Swift, backed by a Brixham sloop, was involved in a running battle with two Revenue cutters, *Alarm* and *Spider*, at Paignton Sands in 1783. The smugglers had the best of the fight, which involved gunfire and serious injuries. *Swift's* crew succeeded in landing 9000 gallons of spirits and four tons of tea. They might well have destroyed the Revenue cutters too, but for support from the Berry Head Battery.

Violence may not be part of the popular image of smugglers, but it was an integral part of the 'free trade'. In 1788, Philip Cumming was badly injured, possibly crippled after being assaulted by smugglers at Hope Cove. His colleague, Philip Cove, had his skull laid bare in the same attack.

As smugglers often carried firearms, it is hardly surprising that they killed their opponents on occasion. In 1798, boatman Humphrey Glynn was shot and killed on board the Cawsand Customs boat when her skipper threatened to board the *Lottery*, a large smuggling cutter. Eventually, the *Lottery* was captured and the culprit hanged.

An alternative to risking their own men and vessels was for the Revenue to use privateers to catch smugglers. Again, the inducement was prize money, but by the very nature of their business, privateers often proved unreliable in their duties. Privateers were vessels licensed by the government to raid enemy shipping. They had long played a significant part in England's wars – especially against the French, who also employed privateers. Whether or not their owners and crew were patriotic, privateers were run for profit. Naturally, their captains were staunch upholders of the free market economy – so much so, that they often used their official trade as a cloak for smuggling.

The Barbican Pool, part of Sutton Harbour at Plymouth, which was a tempting market for smugglers with so many thirsty sailors and ships needing victualling

The government had established a force in 1809 called the Preventative Water Guard. Once Bonaparte was finally crushed in 1815, they were able to divert considerable resources to the fight against smuggling. Captain McCulloch instigated a coastal blockade, recruiting sailors who would otherwise have been pensioned off. Their role was to row small boats close under the cliffs and surprise smugglers landing a cargo. Then they would seize the contraband and claim the prize money.

The blockade continued until 1831, working in conjunction with the Revenue cutters, but it suffered from several inherent weaknesses. In the first place, the Royal Navy did not like the job, which had little lustre to it. Many men deserted, others accepted bribes or even took part in smuggling, as we have seen in the cases of the *Nimble* and the *Rose*.

In 1822 the government created a more unified service by combining the Water Guard with the Revenue cutters and the Riding Officers who had patrolled the coastal paths. This force was called the Coastguard – by which name it is still known today.

In an attempt to reduce the risk of collusion between Water Guards and their friends and relations in the free trade it was ruled that:

> no individual can be appointed to any station within twenty miles of the place of his birth or within twenty miles of the place at which he resided for six months previous to his appointment in the Water Guard.

Although the Coastguard was a better organized and disciplined force than its predecessors and Coastguards were usually armed with two heavy pistols and a cutlass, the job remained a hard and dangerous one. Periods of duty often extended to sixteen hours at a stretch in all winds and weathers and included patrols in an open rowing boat. Lieutenant Henry Shore RN commented on the Coastguard's hard lot: 'It was enough to kill a horse... only a strong man could stand the work!'

By patrolling the land, the Coastguard and its predecessors did much to establish the Coast Path, now a continuous public right of way for over 600 miles between Minehead in Somerset and Swanage in Dorset, including the entire coastline of Devon and Cornwall. Across the Channel in Brittany is the equally beautiful *Sentier des Douaniers* (Customs Officers' Path) along the coast.

Figures published by the government in 1825 show that the combined efforts of the authorities in the first three years of the Coastguard (1822-24) resulted in impressive hauls. Nonetheless, these commodities were considered only a small fraction of the goods that smugglers succeeded in running – for which, of course, no figures are available.

Tobacco	902,684 lb
Snuff	3000 lb
Brandy	135,000 gallons
Rum	253 gallons
Gin	227,000 gallons
Whiskey	10,500 gallons
Tea	19,000 lb
Silks	42,000 yards
India handkerchiefs	2100

As one might expect from resourceful men, the smugglers responded to the new and more efficient Coastguard in a number of ways. One tactic was 'sowing the crop' as previously described. Another was to use smaller, less conspicuous boats for smuggling, such as fishing smacks or coasters, rather than blatant purpose-built smuggling luggers such as *Lottery* and *Swift*. Using foreign vessels, which were largely immune from prosecution in English courts, was also successful.

Smuggling in East Devon

Jack Rattenbury's *Memoirs of a Smuggler* stands alone as a Devon smuggler's autobiography. His picaresque adventures, which include triumphs and disasters, arrests and escapes, spells in prison and voyages legal and illegal across the Channel, to New York, North Africa and elsewhere, begin and end in East Devon. Rattenbury's home village of Beer and his smuggling haunts along the neighbouring coast are brought into close focus, despite the glaring omissions which fear of prosecution forced on him – not to mention his tendency to cast himself as hero.

The East Devon coast was undoubtedly much used by smugglers. Well placed for traffic with the Channel Islands, it also offered many secluded landing places and was closer than other parts of Devon to up-country markets. In 1760 the Collector at the Exeter Custom House made it clear that the men of Beer were established smugglers:

> The greatest part of the smuggling on this coast is carried out by the Beere Boats who generally run their goods on the Western side of the shore of Torbay… lately was landed great quantities of goods; that not less than fifty or sixty men came there and were employed all the night in carrying away the goods, and that most of these men had some kind of offensive weapons or other.

Much more recently (1989), Arthur J Chapple, himself of an old Beer family, published his informative *Beer in Smuggling Times*. This gives several reasons for Beer's prominence in the 'free trade'. One was the long tradition of fishing and boat building. Chapple, whose uncle had been a boat builder, described the sturdy clinker built Beer fishing luggers as ideal for smuggling, being tough, with plenty of beam – and thus plenty of storage space. They were especially good in light winds.

Beer was a close community – perhaps 'closed community' would be apt. Chapple describes it as a 'no go area for foreigners', who were liable to forcible ejection from the village if they aroused suspicion, especially about smuggling, in which virtually everyone was involved. By the same token, any villager who dared betray the smuggling business would have been in real danger. Even the 'brandy pirates', who

The beach at Beer

poached others' sunken casks or casks washed up by the tide, were taking great risks with their neighbours.

Beer Head and White Cliff (where Customs officer John Hurley fell to his death in 1755) were favourite places for light and smoke signals. Chapple thought that the conveniently sited church tower in Beer was probably used for signalling too, whilst the churches in nearby Branscombe, Salcombe Regis, Seaton and Colyton were reputedly hiding places for contraband. Other local hiding places included Bovey House, owned by Rattenbury's patron, Lord Rolle, a cave at Beer Head and two caves in Hooken Undercliff. The extensive underground workings of Beer Quarry caves (open to the public from Easter to September – 01297 680282 for details and charges) were also employed.

Local farmers certainly helped in hiding contraband. In 1953 Clement Ford, Lord of the Manor at Branscombe, showed J RW Coxhead (author of *Smuggling Days in Devon*) six narrow diagonal shafts, which smugglers had driven into the ground in the middle of a field. From skilfully disguised entrances, the shafts led some 12 ft down into chambers 10 ft in diameter.

About the year 1785, a party of smugglers pursued by Revenue officers sank their brandy casks in a pond at Halsbeare Farm near Blackborough in the Blackdown Hills. The incident is reminiscent of the famous Wiltshire smuggling story of the Moonrakers – smugglers who made the pursuing Revenue men think they were harmless fools raking the moonlight, when they were really using their rakes to keep their brandy kegs sunk in a pond.

At Halsbeare Farm, the smugglers escaped, but the suspicious Revenue men dragged the pond and found the casks. Farmer John Frost was accused of aiding the smugglers and his trial was arranged to take place in London – where a conviction was more likely. A heavy fine would have ruined Frost, but his brave daughter, Ellen, rode to London and her evidence cleared Frost's name. She was buried at Kentisbeare in 1821.

As ever, smuggling was a team effort. It was said that 'Sidbury financed, Branscombe landed, Sidmouth found wagons and Salcombe (Salcombe Regis near Sidmouth) carriers.' In modern parlance, the smugglers were excellent at networking. Part of the network was formed by friendly houses on smuggling routes. A row of bottle ends cemented into the wall under the eaves, as at Batts Close on the side of the former Seaton to London coach road, signalled the owner's partiality for smugglers.

Despite the undoubted sailing skills of local smugglers, there is ample proof that smuggling was a dangerous business. The parish registers for Beer and Seaton for the years 1816-25, when smuggling was at its zenith, include a roll of local men reported drowned whilst smuggling. In 1816 alone, five men were recorded.

Seaton church also has an epitaph to the opposition. William Henry Paulson, Midshipman of HMS *Queen Charlotte,* and eight seamen 'perished in a gale of wind off Sidmouth whilst crossing in a galley for the prevention of smuggling in the year 1817'.

Smuggling could be dangerous, but Rattenbury relates an incident at Seaton Hole that was comic:

> Having landed a cargo at Seaton Hole one dark night,
> I was going up the cliff with a keg on my back when I had
> the ill luck to stumble over an ass. It began to bray so
> horribly that, together with noise occasioned by my fall, an
> officer who was taking a nap below awoke, in consequence
> of which he seized nearly forty kegs, being the whole of
> the cargo.

Smuggling in South Devon

Smuggling in South Devon was similar to the free trade in East Devon. The coast between the Exe and the old county boundary at Kingsand/ Cawsand on the west of Plymouth Sound afforded good communications with the Channel Islands and Brittany. It also offered a variety of creeks, coves and beaches for landing contraband.

Dartmouth and Plymouth were usually avoided as landing points. Both were naval stations and home ports for Revenue cutters. However, both ports provided thirsty markets for smuggled goods, especially Plymouth, where it was not unknown for His Majesty's ships to stock up with contraband grog.

Plymouth's handsome new Custom House was built in 1820 facing Sutton Harbour. Both it and its predecessor survived the Plymouth blitz and still stand. The Customs service had long been established in Plymouth by then, as the smugglers had in Cawsand Bay. Smuggling was conducted on a generous scale: in 1804 the Plymouth Collector of Customs estimated that 17,000 casks of spirits were smuggled into Cawsand each year. Three masted luggers and the bigger smuggling cutters could carry up to 800 eight gallon spirit casks, plus tea and tobacco. Fifty smuggling craft were in business at Cawsand by 1815 and a similar number were still employed on French runs in the early 1840s.

By definition, smugglers were mobile and did not necessarily confine themselves to one area, so it is no surprise to find that Jack Rattenbury was active in South Devon. Jack's last smuggling escapade was in 1836, when he and Samuel Pike took a horse and cart with twenty kegs of brandy from Torbay. This was seized at Newton Bushel (now Highweek near Newton Abbot). Pike was caught and jailed. He grassed on Rattenbury and his other accomplices, but the case failed for lack of evidence.

Another who escaped being sent to jail for smuggling in South Devon was Isaac Gulliver. The infamous Dorset smuggler claimed to have retired to Teignmouth in 1782, after he obtained a free pardon through the Act of Oblivion by providing men to serve in the armed forces. As well as conducting a legitimate wine and spirit business in Teignmouth, Gulliver carried on smuggling – very possibly free of prosecution and with the government's tacit approval in return for providing information about the French.

Dawlish Warren, the spit of sand extending into the mouth of the Exe east of Teignmouth, was a favoured landing place for contraband. Another landing place nearby was just below the rock stacks known as the Parson and Clerk. A lane winds up from there to Holcombe, where smugglers cut caves into the sandstone cliffs. Unfortunately, these caves were destroyed when the railway was constructed in 1846. Another piece of smuggling history was partly lost when the Mount Pleasant Inn was badly damaged by fire in 1955, but happily this was rebuilt on the old pattern.

The coast from Shaldon to Torbay was also well known for smuggling, as the names Brandy Cove, Smuggler's Hole and Smuggler's Cove indicate. Other beaches known to have been used by smugglers in this area include Anstey's Cove, Oddicombe, Watcombe Beach, Maidencombe, Labrador Bay and the Ness beach at Shaldon.

Rocombe Farm and Maidencombe Farm, which had a trapdoor leading to a secret chamber, were among the hiding places for contraband in the area. The Combe Cellars, an isolated inn at Combeinteignhead on the Teign Estuary was an ideal smuggling depot; vessels could be unloaded directly into its cellars.

The Combe Cellars is far from being the only Devon inn claiming

Above: Kingsand, now in Cornwall but formerly in Devon

Below: The Coombe Cellars inn might have been built for smugglers – and perhaps it was!

a smuggling connection. Another is the Pilchard on Burgh Island opposite Bigbury. Said to date from 1336, it used to have a skull and crossbones on the sign. The Pilchard was the haunt of smuggler Tom Crocker, who was eventually discovered and shot outside the inn by the excisemen.

At Ringmore between Bigbury and Kingston is the Journey's End. Smugglers are said to have hidden their contraband in a secret room behind a false wall of the inn. A few miles west at Bantham is an inn called the Sloop, recalling the one-masted fore and aft rigged vessel much used by 18th century excisemen such as the Collector, Warren Lisle, whose sloop *Cholmondeley* was based at Exeter. Sloops were also used by the Royal Navy as small ships of war and recognized for their manoeuvrability and speed.

The west-facing coast between Prawle Point and Wembury offered a number of fairly secluded landing places favoured by smugglers – especially the Yealm estuary, the Avon estuary and Hope Cove. Ralph's Hole, a fissure in the cliffs on Bolberry Down near Hope Cove, was named after a smuggler who kept the preventive men at bay with a pitchfork.

The area is notorious for shipwrecks. Smuggler Philip Kingcup and all his crew were drowned when they were wrecked at the Mewstone by Bolt Head. Their vessel was washed ashore along the coast at Hope Cove with Kingcup's brandy kegs still slung around her, ready for sinking.

Smuggling continues, not least along this part of the coast. In 1980, a smuggling vessel was damaged at Hope Cove. Staying at the Hope and Anchor, the smugglers unloaded a ton and a half of cannabis and hid it in a cave. They were caught after loading the drugs into a lorry.

Between Start Point and Dartmouth, the shingle beaches would seem ideal for landing – they were used as practice beaches in 1944 for the D-Day landings. No records have survived to substantiate a smuggling connection, but Rev. Sabine Baring Gould recounted an amusing tale of one Sir Thomas ———, whose stately home near Dartmouth was searched for contraband. The best efforts of the preventive men failed to detect any. They should have looked in the family coach, which was so full of smuggled goods its axles had to be supported by stands.

A more outrageous smuggling story concerns 'Resurrection' Bob Elliott of Brixham. It is said that Bob was once laid up with a bad

Above: The Journey's End at Ringmore

Below: Hope Cove

Bayard's Cove at Dartmouth

attack of gout (seemingly an occupational hazard for the bibulous smugglers), when his colleagues hid a quantity of contraband in his cottage. The preventive men were suspicious and paid Bob a visit, but were told he had died during the night. Out of respect for his grieving family, they forbore to search the property.

An exceptionally large coffin was brought to take Bob on his last journey – but then, he was an exceptionally large man. When a party of coastguards met a funeral procession on the Brixham to Totnes road that night, they were about to ask a few questions when they encountered the ghost of Bob at the rear and fled.

When the coastguards reported the incident to their sceptical commander the next day, he determined to revisit Bob Elliott's cottage. As he eavesdropped by Bob's window he was mortified to hear the man himself telling his friends how he had duped the preventive men. Storming into the house, the officer gave Bob a severe reprimand – but left it at that, perhaps ashamed of the way his men had been so easily fooled.

Smuggling in North Devon

The rocky north coast of Devon was a different proposition from any part of the south coast. Less closely watched by the authorities than the south because smugglers used it less, it suffered the major disadvantage of facing away from France and the Channel Islands, the main sources of supply. Shipping contraband around Land's End was difficult, slow and dangerous. However, North Devon offered smugglers some excellent opportunities, which they exploited with entrepreneurial skill.

Merchant ships from all corners of the world sailed up the Bristol Channel. Skippers wanting to sell their dutiable cargoes before reaching Customs at Bristol found the men of North Devon, especially those operating from Lundy, eager to help. The Dutch captains of East Indiamen carrying tea and tobacco and the English crews of West Indiamen carrying rum and other goods particularly appreciated this service.

By 1700, Bideford, supported by Barnstaple, was second only to London as a tobacco port. It thus offered a variety of smuggling prospects. One was to import the cargo legitimately, claim 'drawback' on tobacco duties (stating the goods were being re-exported) and then smuggle them back into England. Another technique was to offload the tobacco into small boats and bypass Customs altogether.

Lundy, on the shipping lane to Bristol, had long been a stronghold for smugglers and pirates. It was ideally placed for Bideford smugglers, handy without being so close to the port as to be easily observed. There was room for large quantities of contraband. With fortifications and only one landing place, it was very secure.

In 1748 Thomas Benson acquired the lease on Lundy. Benson was a local shipping magnate, Sheriff of Devon and Member of Parliament. He also enjoyed a lucrative contract to ship convicts to Virginia (which was used as a dumping ground for England's undesirables before the American Revolution) at £20 a head. His vessels then returned with valuable cargoes of tobacco.

With Lundy in his pocket, Benson saw a way to increase his profits. He shipped his convicts only as far as Lundy and made them work on developing the island's fortifications and storage facilities, including 'Benson's Cave'. They also worked at sorting the duty-free tobacco into smaller packages and smuggling it back into small places such as Clovelly.

After eight Lundy convicts had escaped and made it ashore at Hartland Quay, suspicions were aroused. Benson was tried before the House of Lords, as well as receiving demands for £8300 from the Board in London for smuggling tobacco back to the mainland.

With his affairs in this parlous state, the impenitent Benson arranged an insurance scam. In July 1752, he unloaded his heavily insured vessel *Nightingale* at Lundy, sailed her a little further west and scuttled her. Once safely ashore again with his crew, Benson submitted his insurance claim. A seaman talked and Benson made a lucky escape to Portugal, leaving the master of *Nightingale* to face trial and execution. Our hero continued trading from Portugal and died peacefully in 1771. An Appledore restaurant was recently named in his honour.

Lundy continued as a fortified smuggling depot, as later raids by Customs officers from both North Devon and South Wales proved. However, with well over one hundred miles of coastline, the county's north coast offered many other small ports and coves for landing contraband. These were widely exploited.

The thinly populated Exmoor coast was well suited to smuggling. R D Blackmore in *Lorna Doone* (1869) described how smugglers 'land

Chambercombe Manor, on the outskirts of Ilfracombe. One explanation for the haunted reputation of this and a number of other locations is that it suited smugglers if people were scared to go out at night

their goods without regard to the King's Revenue at the little haven of Lynmouth'. The medieval Rising Sun by the harbour and the adjacent cottages on Mars Hill – handily equipped with ample salting houses for storing contraband – were associated with the free trade.

Brandy Cove just west of Ilfracombe's harbour was used by smugglers, as its name suggests. (There is another Brandy Cove at Torquay.) So too was Samson's Bay, just east of Ilfracombe, where a smuggler called Samson used the cave in the cliff for storage. A mile south of the town, Chambercombe Manor (reputedly one of the most haunted houses in Devon) may also have been used for storing contraband. Certainly, it has a hidden room and a really chilling ghost story is told on the guided tour. (Open Easter to end October, Monday to Friday, plus Sunday afternoons. 01271 862624 www.chambercombemanor. co.uk)

Smuggler's Leap near Martinhoe, between Ilfracombe and Lynmouth, is said to gain its name from the pursuit of a smuggler by a preventive officer. Both were on horseback and both plunged to their deaths over the cliff, one struggling for freedom, the other for justice.

A storm brewing over Braunton Burrows. As on the South Devon coast, the sea itself was often the greatest danger to smugglers.

In 1791, the armed Fowey smuggling vessel Abeona *was driven ashore at Northam Burrows on the other side of the Taw/Torridge estuary. The preventive men seized £5000 worth of contraband, including 700 ankers of spirits, tea, tobacco, silk, china and playing cards.*

After landing 96 tubs of brandy at Heddon's Mouth, the smuggling cutter Hope *was wrecked at Watermouth Bay in 1799 in an attempt to land a further 80 tubs. All the crew were lost*

When the seaweed gatherers discovered them, they were still locked together in deadly combat.

Heddon's Mouth near Martinhoe was certainly used by smugglers, for twenty ankers of spirits and thirteen bales of tobacco were found there by preventive men in 1786. Other discoveries at that time focused on the Taw/Torridge estuary. In 1782, the Revenue cutter *Scorpion* seized fifty ankers of brandy, 150lb of tobacco and four bags of tea on the beach at Northam Burrows. The following year, the Tidewaiter found 210 casks of spirits and a quantity of tobacco close to Instow Quay.

Conclusion

The hazard of shipwreck was something all sailors had to live with to a far greater degree in the 18th and early 19th centuries than now. It was accepted as one of the risks of the smuggling trade, along with fines, imprisonment and the destruction of smuggling vessels by the authorities.

The end of the road? For most convicted smugglers, a prison hulk was more likely to be a stepping stone to transportation, or to enforced service in the Royal Navy

Even the imposition of the death penalty for smuggling by the Acts of 1736 and 1746 had limited results. After all, smuggling was generally much more lucrative than the host of other capital crimes. Some risked the gallows for stealing goods valued at only one shilling.

Smuggling continued on a large scale as long as high duties made it profitable. When these duties were reduced, the classic era of smuggling drew to a close around 1850. Drastically reduced profits meant that few would take the risks involved in smuggling.

Smugglers still use the coast of Devon. In the later 20th century, the increased market for illegal narcotics opened a new smuggling era with the potential for enormous profits. With a large scale international criminal organisation and modern communications, it has a very different character from smuggling in the 18th and early 19th centuries. Then, contraband involved exorbitantly taxed, but generally accepted goods. Now, smuggling is focused largely (but not exclusively) on narcotics which most people agree should never be traded.